FROM THE

D0863100

Making the Small Church Grow

Making the
Small Church Grow

by
Robert E. Maner

Beacon Hill Press of Kansas City
Kansas City, Missouri

Lovingly dedicated
to
My wife, *Jewell,* who
not only typed this
manuscript, but has
helped me and has
been a chief source
of inspiration for
30 years.

Contents

Foreword

Any pastor who *wants* his church to grow will find in this meaty little volume both hope and practical instruction—along with an occasional spiritual prod! It is a book he can ill afford not to buy and read.

This is not just another study on church growth; it is a disarmingly simple but eminently helpful book written by a small-church pastor who has earned his right to speak. It comes from the mind and heart of a practitioner who has seen his own congregation almost double in the past few years and come alive in the spirit of servanthood to Christ and its community. It breathes a spirit of pastoral concern born of love for God and people, and I predict it will rekindle in you new hope and fresh vision for your church.

Robert E. Maner was a bright student in my classes, and he has remained a student. He has kept abreast of church growth literature and listened to the experts. But this book is no mere regurgitation of others' ideas; its freshness and strength lie in its originality, pertinency and urgency.

This book is well written. It skillfully unmasks fallacious assumptions which sometimes lull smaller churches to sleep. It punctures the false pride which so easily besets such congregations. It also flashes with insights and sparkles with illustrations.

Above all, if you are a beleaguered and bewildered small-church pastor, these pages should lift your spirits, clarify your vision, give you a new sense of dignity and self-worth in your assignment and motivate you to rethink your ministry, reorder your priorities and reorganize your church.

I predict a long and useful ministry for this book, and I am happy to commend it to you.

WILLIAM M. GREATHOUSE
General Superintendent

Preface

Pastors of small churches are a special breed. Most of them have a sort of inferiority complex that goes with the job. Actually there is nothing disgraceful about being a small-church pastor. Most of the churches in this world are small churches. In fact, the large church is a very rare exception. But it is the large church that we hear about most of the time. It is the pastor of the large church who is always telling us how and what to do. It is his church that is always in the news. Therefore, we get the idea that he is the only one doing anything. Or at least he is the only one doing anything right.

Actually, that whole concept is very far from the truth. The small-church pastor has no cause to be ashamed. It is not the small church that is the failure but the church that is not growing. A church may be ever so large and barely holding its own—even shrinking—while a neighboring church may be much smaller and growing rapidly. Which church and pastor should be considered a success? It is not the small church but the static church that should have the inferior feelings.

Perhaps a definition of terms is appropriate here. By *small church* we will use the definition "a church with an average attendance at its maximum service of 200 or less." That could mean Sunday School or morning worship or whatever else occasionally may exceed that number. It means a membership of less than 200 and a paid staff of only one full-time employee. It may have a part-time secretary and a part-time custodian. It could mean a part-time minister of music or youth. But for our definition: less than 200 members, less than 200 average attendance, and one full-time pastor with only part-time assistance.

This particular limit may not be appropriate for some denominations. But for the sake of clarity for those who will likely read these pages, these will be the factors that constitute the small church. It is essentially a one-man operation. These limitations are imposed by a number of possible reasons: a genuine lack of additional money; the unwillingness of the church to employ additional assistance for the pastor; the church not feeling that the pastor needs paid assistants to accomplish his task; or rarely, the reluctance of the pastor to work with additional staff members. But, whatever the reason, the pastor is basically doing the whole job as far as full-time employees are concerned. Volunteer help and some limited part-time paid assistance carry the full operation of the church.

A vast majority of Protestant churches fit into the category described. In fact, very many churches do not even have a full-time pastor. Their minister is either a bivocational pastor or a student at some nearby school.

Perhaps the author of these pages has but one qualification for undertaking such an enterprise: For 30 years I have been the pastor of just such a church as that described. Most books on church growth and the pastoral ministry are written by the pastors of the large churches. Some are written by men in administrative positions who are former pastors of large churches. But I have yet to see a book written by the pastor of a small church on how to pastor a small church. The church I now serve is just below crossing the boundaries described for defining a small church. I have watched it grow from a group of little more than 100 to a group with an average attendance of almost 200. If the growth pattern of the past four years can be continued, we will leave the category of the small church before these words ever see print. So I want to write this while I am still in the midst of the problems that are peculiar to the pastor of the small church.

Small churches have problems that are unique because of their size. Pastors of these churches are under pressures that are soon forgotten by men who have graduated to something bigger. Once these pressures are forgotten, it is easy to become unsympathetic to the men still struggling with frustrating situations created by the size and limitation of the church. I am still in the midst of that pressure. I know that larger churches have their problems, too. Maybe they have even more difficulties. But I am not writing for them. This book is addressed to the small-church pastor and people and problems. It is, in effect, a "what we did to solve it" book. Like Edison in his search for a filament to make a light bulb, I found a thousand ways *not* to do it. My years of trial and error have produced a few workable ideas. If they will help some other pastor and congregation get the job done more quickly and more efficiently, this shall be sufficient for my efforts.

1
The Quality of the Small Church

Church growth is the big thing these days. We hear it at every convention. We see books in every religious bookstore on "How to Make Your Church Grow" or a kindred theme. Actually growth is not all there is to a church. Church growth should be the result of something with a higher motive than just having a larger church than someone else. And when we get to the place that all we want is growth for growth's sake, we are no better than a cancer cell. This is its purpose for growth too. Growth should be the natural result of the efficient operation of a church that is doing a superior job. When we start doing a superior job, a church will grow. Maybe our problem lies right in this spot. What we should concentrate on is not growth but quality ministry.

Quality does not mean withdrawing ourselves into a little monastic order of secluded saints who fear visitors and see them as intruders. It does not mean developing an attitude of repulsive superiority. By quality, we are thinking of the ability to meet the needs of the people we have some contact with. It means finding out where people hurt and relieving that pain. It means finding a need and filling it. And above all, it means having a church that offers high quality in every point of the operation of that church.

I was an evangelist for three years. In that time I preached in many small churches. I worked with small-church pastors and their people. In all kindness, I must say that I saw some things that were disastrous to church growth and progress. I saw things that made it virtually impossible for the church to grow. Usually, if the pastor asked me, I would make some helpful observations. Most of the time I just quietly suffered through it all until my turn came and then preached the best I could under the circumstances. But I learned a lot in those years. When I reentered the pastoral ministry, I was a much wiser pastor. An objective look at the church proved to be most helpful in my own ministry.

Now, nine years later, I have had opportunity to try some of the theories I developed in those days. Many have been dropped; others have proven successful. The third category is comprised of those that will not work for me in my situation, but still hold hope for others in their churches. These have been carefully filed for another day.

However, having stated the need for quality, we should not be satisfied for our church to remain the same size year after year. If we have done the best we can to provide quality, but growth still does not occur, other steps will be required. Growth should occur as the result of a quality ministry. But the rate of growth must be sufficient to more than offset the losses. It is lack of recognition of this fact that causes a church to hit a level and stop growing. We reach about 100 average in Sunday School attendance and can't get beyond that figure. We bounce around over a margin of 25, plus or minus, for the next 25 years. Pastors come and go and the church remains the same. Some pastors do better than others, but essentially the church stays the same size year after year.

What is wrong? Why do churches quit growing? They build a new building, hoping that this will bring in the people. But, to their dismay, they find the average attendance is lower in the fine, new church than it was in the old, ragged building they vacated. The new building with the much higher mortgage payments didn't help the church grow at all.

The church and pastor develop what has appropriately been named "the postbuilding blues." The pastor and people have both been through a lot getting the new building erected. There were the endless meetings with the architect and contractors. There were many meetings with bankers and building committees. After months of waiting and working to finish the big building project, there finally came the exciting day when the congregation moved in for the first service. Some months after that came the dedication service with some church leader present for the service. Maybe city officials sat in the congregation. What a great time it was for the church!

Sadly, all of this did not continue. Everyone who

came from here and there to help this congregation celebrate the occasion went home. The little congregation is now left all alone. The normal emotional backlash sets in. Some who didn't like the way things were done begin to complain. Others who did not get their way in choices and selections begin picking at flaws. It doesn't take long for this kind of situation to develop some real sour members.

The pastor is now very discouraged. The people begin to sense his discouragement, and they follow their leader. The whole group sits there in a beautiful, new church that they should be very proud of, on a lovely, new piece of property in the better section of town with everything nice and new. But what happens? They begin fussing and squabbling over petty details. The pastor resigns! The church is not standing still now, it is losing members.

If only the pastor had anticipated this "postbuilding blues" syndrome and planned for a program to offset it, he might still be there, enjoying the new building he worked so hard to help provide. If the people had had something else to go on to, they would be seeing the new church house the growing congregation they expected. But it is all lost because there was no challenging program to avoid the backlash and emotional letdown after a building program.

Many pastors and church boards have gone through all of this. Leaders attend church growth seminars, have study courses, and read all of the current books, of which there are so many. What is wrong?

The remaining pages will be the story of what one church and pastor did. It will rub some the wrong way. It will deal with some attitudes that we don't like to admit having. But the facts are there. When they are faced honestly and squarely, they can be overcome. But not until then.

2

The Attitude of the Small Church

Why do so many churches fail to grow? It is really not that hard a question to answer. That may sound like an oversimplification, but it is not. There are two major possible answers to that question. One, they don't know how. Second, they don't want to. The response to the first alternative is dealt with in later chapters. But that second option is the one that hurts. And that is the one that must be dealt with first.

Is it possible that we have so many churches that do not grow because they do not want to? We talk about growth; we pray about growth; we have revivals to reach new people. Church boards send their pastors across the country to study growth. We have spent so much money and time on church growth; is it possible that all of this is done by people who down deep in their hearts do not want what they seem to be seeking?

The answer to this is both yes and no. Many church members and some pastors do not know they don't want church growth. They think they want their churches to grow; but they really don't. If someone would ask them, they would, for the most part, never admit this negative attitude. An even bigger tragedy is that they will not admit it even to themselves. They have convinced themselves that they would like to see their church functioning as a large, efficient organization doing quality work for God. But in reality, they want it just like it is. That is why it *is* just like it is.

The question comes to mind: "Why do we church members and pastors fear and resist growth?" We fear it because people fear change. And change is essential if growth is to occur. No church can remain the same if it grows. And since change is not wholly predictable, the result is secret hostility to the very thing we profess to want. The final result is failure. And however we may justify failure, it is still failure.

A scapegoat is usually the best way to discharge guilt over failure. We look around and try to find some excuse for the reason we have failed. We talk about high standards, in spite of the fact that other churches with more stringent membership requirements are growing. We point to the unpopularity of holiness in spite of the fact that some other holiness churches are growing. The scapegoat list is endless; why pursue it?

If growth is to occur, most churches will have to begin with the prevailing attitude. This attitude that must be dealt with may take one of two forms. It can be either positive hostility to growth or negative pessimism. Frequently both attitudes may be present in the same congregation; sometimes in the same people. I have heard church members declare, "Our church is big enough." That is positive hostility. Others will say, "We have been trying for 20 years, and we are still the same size." The implication is, "We will be the same size for the next 20 years."

So if the churches are to grow to the size that will make it possible for them to offer a quality ministry, we must begin with the minds of the people in that church. It must happen in their thinking before it can ever happen in fact.

The resourceful pastor will begin preaching on the subject of growth. He will preach frequently on the unreached harvest fields about the church. He will gather some pertinent facts about the community where his church is located. He will keep this theme before the people. But it will take a lot more than that. Most of the members have been hearing pastors and evangelists preach on that for years—preaching and then doing nothing about it. This kind of apathy after a sermon does more harm than good. Each time it gets a little harder to get the same response in hands raised promising to do this or that—promises that both preacher and people know they will never keep. So the pastor will have to be aware of the calloused consciences he is trying to penetrate. But preach he must; this is the place to start. But he cannot be assured a lot will happen just because a sermon is preached on the subject.

Most of us have heard the story of the old zoo keeper who retired after so very many years of tending the elephant. For a generation he had taken the elephant out to the same stake and chained him to it with the same old chain. The elephant walked around the same stake in the same path year after year with the same old chain dragging along behind him. But the old man retired, and the new man came on the job. On the first day he took the old elephant out to the same old stake but didn't know about the chain, so none was attached. But it didn't matter because the elephant went on walking right in the same old path without ever realizing the chain was gone. The chain was now in the elephant's mind. And he was bound just as surely as if it had been around his leg.

Most of our chains are in our minds. They are just as real as those of forged steel. They hold us just as certainly to the same old path year after year as we go round and round. In like manner we have forged some chains that now bind us. Until these are broken, it is not likely that we will deviate from the familiar path. Admittedly, chain breaking can be painful and sometimes very difficult work. But they must be broken.

The chains that bind us are also a source for our feeling of security. So chain cutting will win no popularity awards. Some will see this effort as an attack on them rather than a blessing to them. These are old, familiar friends we are slaying. They have been our crutch to lean on. They have been our smoke screen to hide behind for lo, these many years. They will not be easily parted with. There may be chains far more numerous than the few listed here.

1. The chain of *smallness:* The thinking is, we have to be a small church; we can never grow to any great extent beyond the size we are now. In reality the truth is, that, with some exceptions, every church can become a church approaching the size of the larger churches in our towns or communities. If they did it, so can we if we want to. The size of church we think we are limited to is all in our minds. We must change our minds before we can change our size.

2. The chain of *denominational label:* How many times we have heard it said, "If we would change our church name to thus and so, I guarantee we could be big like them." Not if we do not do what they are doing, we wouldn't! And if we will do what they are doing, we could be as big with any name.

3. Another strong chain is that of the *pastor as prophet, priest, and errand boy:* Most church members would not own up to it; but really, down in their hearts, they think their pastor should be the church flunky. They think he ought to be the building custodian, operate the mimeograph machine, run a free taxi, keep the church yards clean, and do anything else that others choose to neglect. Now most pastors of small churches do these things automatically. They too just take it for granted that it is part of the job of being pastor. Besides, if they didn't do it, it would never get done. The pastor's wife joins him in those numerous tasks that should be shared by all but

seldom are. This chain will be hard to cut, but it too will have to go.

4. The chain of *inferiority:* Somehow we have gotten it into our minds that other churches are made up of members who are all nine feet tall. Like the Israelites, we keep seeing how big the giants are and how small all of us "grasshoppers" look. Those big churches with the "mile-high" steeples down on the courthouse square have problem people too. In fact, they have problems that would make ours look mighty small. Their members are not all supermen. We will have to convince our congregations that we are as capable as anybody. We will have to be convinced that we can do anything anybody else can do—maybe more.

5. The chain of *spiritual pride:* How people can feel inferior and still be guilty of spiritual pride is a paradox that I have never been able to understand. But it is very real, and it does exist in many churches. It would seem that if we are superior spiritually, we would be superior. If we are inferior, then it would seem that we are inferior in spiritual matters also. Not so! It is possible for the members of a little congregation to draw self-righteous robes about themselves and almost dare a visitor to come among them. Then they can justify their dwarfed size by this excuse: "They just won't pay the price." What price are they talking about? The price of battering the door down?

Yet this same little dried-up congregation will affirm, "We don't expect to be big like other churches. We can't do what they are doing." At least they are right in that analysis. They can't be big like other churches unless they have some radical changes.

There are many chains that are unique to the local situation of a given congregation. The pastor must find these chains that bind the minds of the people and with loving hands begin to break them. He must show the members that it is not a choice between being big or being spiritual. New members in large numbers will not bring in a lot of undesirable practices if the proper safeguards are taken. Besides, being small is no guarantee either that a church can retain its original spirituality or religious vitality. Contrariwise, being small places that church that much nearer to total extinction. If a few members die and others move away, it would be all over for the church. That has happened; and it can happen rather quickly. A larger church always has a better chance of survival and, really, a better chance of preserving its spiritual heritage.

So let us break the chains! Let the old elephant walk in some new paths. He just might like it.

3
The Structure of the Small Church

My father was a boilermaker for the railroad. He worked on the old steam engines that are so much a symbol of the railroads of an earlier day. Back in the late 40s, after World War II, the railroads replaced their steam engines with the new diesel locomotives. When the steam engines went, my father's job went with them. They didn't need boilermakers if they had no boilers. The big day came when they had all the old steel locomotives lined up at the roundhouse to be hauled away and cut up as scrap. It was a sad day for those of us who grew up around the railroad tracks to think they were to be forever gone. It was the passing of an era. I went down to see the sad sight. It was like a funeral.

The old roundhouse had been there for who knows how long. In front of it was a fishpond that had been there for about the same length of time. Swimming around in that pond were goldfish over a foot long. I never saw such large goldfish in my life. When I went inside, I asked the old gentleman in the office where they found such large goldfish. All the goldfish I had ever seen were about two inches long. "Oh," he replied, "those are no special kind. They are just like any other." Seeing my surprise, he went on to explain, "You put your fish in a little fishbowl. They stay little. If you put them in a big pond like that one, they will in time be just as big as those are."

Now, I don't know much about fish, but that did make sense. In fact, it makes sense in more ways than one. If that is true of fish, it just could be true of other things. Maybe the size of the container does control the size of the contents more than we think. An oak tree planted in a flowerpot would never become a great tree no matter how long anyone watered it and watched it grow. It would always be a little dwarf of a plant, never able to reach its full potential.

Churches are not fish or oak trees, but there might be a lesson here that churches can learn. If a church is going to grow, it will have to be put together so that the structure does not make it impossible for it to grow. The organizational structure will either aid or restrict growth. When it comes to outgrowing the building, it is easy to decide when the need arises to enlarge. If people are sitting on the floor or standing around the walls, it can be safely said, "It's time for a building program." But it is not always so easy to see when the organizational structure of the church has been outgrown, but this too can limit growth. And no one will even realize what the problem of arrested growth really is.

Is there not a lesson in a child stacking blocks? One

on another, the tottering stack rises. The higher it gets, the more uncertain its future becomes. Then the predictable calamity happens—down they fall. Little wonder! If the child ever hopes to have a stack that goes very high, he will have to do the thing that is obvious to us. He will have to build a much bigger base. The bigger the base, the higher he will be able to stack the blocks.

Even a child can eventually figure that one out. Why then could we not have figured that out when building church organizations? Why has it taken so long for us to see why we can't build big churches on such a limited base? The builders of the pyramids did their work a very long time ago. All of us have been looking at their designs all of our lives. How is it that we never came up with the simple conclusion, "Let's build churches like the pyramids!"

Churches that have grown to be giant congregations have done so because they, for the most part, were planned that way. The builders started out with that in mind. They got a base broad enough to support what they planned to put on top. They designed their church organization with the idea that it would have to be so planned that unlimited growth would be possible. As the churches grew, so did the organization. When organization restricted growth, this fact was detected and adjustments were made to eliminate the problem.

Now what are we talking about where churches are concerned? Just this. If any church is to grow beyond the small group of friends who get together each Sunday to sing and pray and then hear its dear little pastor deliver a message to the faithful few, it will have to plan for that growth. This will mean organizing so that it will happen. This means a dedication to the principles that will make it happen. This means giving up the Sunday afternoon nap and the Saturday afternoon golf games. This will mean more than tithing and giving a quarter in the Sunday School offering. This will mean more than nodding through that little message the dear pastor is trying to preach.

It will mean getting to church an hour early and staying an hour late. It will mean laymen taking on responsibilities that laymen have never had to carry before. It will mean reading books, taking study courses, visiting all through the week, getting under the real load of the church burden. It will mean a hundred things that laymen have never done before. It will mean doing it gladly, with real joy in our hearts for the privilege of the job.

Now, here is the shocker! There are laypeople that are just looking for a church that will so challenge them and motivate them into doing just that. I can just hear a lot of pastors saying, "I wish I had even a few people in my church like you have described! That is what I need!" Not necessarily so! What many a pastor needs is to get the people in his church so excited about the church that they will keep him hopping trying to find jobs for them to do.

Sad to say, I cannot visualize getting very excited about what I have seen happening in the average small church. There is often nothing there to get excited about. The singing is dead and the people deader. The service is one long drag. I have been in some churches that made me wonder why anybody came. I deeply pitied the few poor souls who had nothing better to look forward to Sunday after Sunday. I am not sure that I would do as well as they are doing under similar circumstances.

When we are willing to dig down to the very foundation and restructure our church program with the potential for something exciting, then something exciting will begin to happen. New people will be attracted to the church. New faces bring excitement. New people will mean new energy, new life, and new ideas. An organization can begin to evolve that will create the possibility for endless expansion and growth. Each stage will have to be planned and implemented with the same care and enthusiasm.

One final observation on the concept of this kind of foundation. Time! It will take time. The unwise pastor who thinks he can make this happen in a few months is headed for trouble. Occasionally, someone might find a situation that is just right for sweeping changes of this nature. But for most of us, it will take several years. I am entering my fifth year, and we still have growing pains. The two-year pastor might just as well stop reading now. If that is one's usual tenure of service, such a man will have to find help elsewhere. These things will take time and patience and a lot of love. But for the man who is willing to plan for the years ahead with his congregation, the only limit placed on him is his own willingness to work.

Excitement always draws a crowd. When the pastor gets excited, he can get his people excited. When they get excited, he had better start thinking about a building program. They will crowd you out. And the people, not the pastor, are the only ones who can really build a great church. For the people are the church. The pastor is but the shepherd. And sheep are the ones who should reproduce sheep.

4

The Ministry of the Small Church

All that has been stated so far has been introductory. These basic concepts stated include a right attitude on the part of pastor and people and a right structure. We need now to discuss the matter of building a structure that will allow growth.

THE CHAIN OF COMMAND

Perhaps it would be best to mention the importance of the chain of command at the beginning, even though it will, of necessity, be developed as the entire organization grows. At first it will be a matter of working with two or three people. But the idea of this working through channels needs to be planned for and taught right from the beginning. Later, as the organization grows, it will become extremely important. Just as the pyramid is stacked one stone on another until it reaches the pinnacle, so a well-organized church will, in the end, look structurally just like a pyramid. Each stone will bear the weight its position demands, but all will be directed toward the peak. If the people of the church are taught that they really do have an important place of responsibility, they are far more likely to take their position seriously. If the pastor respects these people and insists that others do likewise, they will feel they have real authority.

One advantage that a church has over a pyramid is that the base can be expanded as the structure goes up. In fact, the whole structure will grow together, moving up and out at the same time.

Developing the Small-Group Ministry

The small-group ministry is an asset toward growth as well as a quality ministry to people. The importance of keeping our ministry as a "ministry to people" cannot be overemphasized. People is what the church is all about.

People must always be primary in the whole organization. People, real people, with names and faces, people with children and homes—that is the church. Neither programs nor organizations must ever take precedence over the people that make up the church. Everything is organized around people. Everything is done to help people know Jesus Christ a little better. People! Nothing should ever crowd them out of the picture.

This is why the small-group ministry is so important. Many people can't handle the situation created by a large crowd where they become anonymous. They can relate to a Sunday School class of 10 or 15. They feel lost if all they ever meet at church is an audience of 200 or 300 every time they enter the door. They can't identify with a vast congregation of people, mostly strangers. They feel like visitors every time they come. So the small-group ministry must be developed and maintained throughout the church.

1. The Sunday School is divided into departments. These, in turn, are divided into classes. These classes are usually not allowed to get too large. This is the custom in almost every church. Why not make this a way of life for everything else in the church? If it works in Sunday School, we can make it work elsewhere.

2. Pastors can handle the small group much easier.

3. People can find a place of meaningful service better in a small group.

4. Most people are accustomed to small groups. The family is a small group. People can learn the names of those in a small group and make friends far more readily. Later, when the whole congregation is assembled in the church sanctuary for the morning worship service, they see John and Mary sitting over there, and they can go sit with them. They no longer feel so lost in the crowd, now that they have friends they know and with whom they like to sit.

There are many good and valid reasons for having as many small groups functioning in your church as you can possibly organize. They can meet at various times and places as need and choice will dictate.

How Can We Develop a Small-Group Ministry?

Since the church is people oriented, the small groups will be built around the needs of the people. What the people need and want will to a large extent tell you what groups to organize. Also the makeup of the church will cause considerable variety from church to church. When I pastored in Texas several years ago, my wife organized a ladies fellowship that was very successful. The ladies in that particular church enjoyed getting together in that capacity. They found great pleasure on those special occasions like Christmas and Thanksgiving in dressing up in long dresses and, with their husbands, really having a delightful party. This met their need and afforded an opportunity for them to bring their friends into a church situation they could be proud of.

My present church is made up of a large number of young married people. They too enjoy getting together. But they enjoy playing volleyball in a mixed group with husbands and wives both participating much better than a fancy party. The ladies fellowship idea just has not caught on here like it did in other places. So, we try to meet the needs of the people. It is pointless to force people to attend and participate in things they have little or no interest in.

The point is, the needs and interests will to a large extent determine the number and nature of small groups operating in the church. If we begin with a set of fixed, inflexible notions, we will greatly limit our potential success. If we are willing to let the church grow like a tree, we will see limbs shooting out all over the place. Granted, we will have to give some guidance and direction. Certainly, we will give spiritual guidance when things that are not compatible with the Christian life and the Bible are suggested. Not everything that might be suggested will be approved. There will always be some pruning to do. But ideas should be considered for the sake of the person making the suggestion. We ought to show him that much respect.

Another word of caution is needed here. We never begin a project or program until we are reasonably certain that we can see it through. The world is full of starters. They get all excited about some pet project they hear of in another church. There is much talk and making of big plans for an exciting new enterprise. Then a month later its promoters are not to be found. It is all forgotten, and a lot of people are hurt and disappointed. Before we begin any new small group, we try to make certain that we have dependable, dedicated leadership that will stay with the undertaking and see it to a successful conclusion. We also make sure that the project will either pay its own way or that money has been appropriated for its operation.

WHAT ARE THESE SMALL GROUPS?

Basically, the small-group ministry can be classified into two categories. There is the conventional and there is the special. For example, we all have Sunday School with classes. Each class is a small group. Most churches have some kind of youth group organization. Then there is the necessary organization of the church with a church board which has trustees and stewards. Actually, each of these constitutes a small group which has real meaning to those who serve on it. There is the missionary society, children's church, Caravan (or Scouting), and several other very basic and traditional auxiliaries operating in the church.

What is being suggested here is that we capitalize on these already existing groups. We should give them real meaning and identity, utilizing their usefulness as a group of people serving in this small setting. For example, the choir is a small group. That choir should have some group spirit. The members should take pride in the fact that they are in the choir; they should want to be a good choir. When new people come into the church who can sing, they should be involved in the choir. This is a small group they can relate to. Most people who can sing enjoy doing so. Immediately this new person feels a part of the group. He belongs! He has found a nest. If this approach can be followed throughout the entire church, there will be few strangers at the church, no matter how large the church becomes.

It would be pointless to elaborate on the organization of the Sunday School or the missionary society or other basic and traditional groups. There are many books available, telling us how to do this. One word, however, does seem appropriate: division! If the missionary society is broken up into chapters, they can meet as small groups at different times and places, and they will begin to feel some identity of their own.

This is important. If every organization within the church is reduced to small groups, they can undertake projects and sponsor campaigns in far greater number than one large group that meets in the church sanctuary, say on a Wednesday night, for their monthly missionary meeting.

Not only does the average church have the basic small groups already in existence and operating in the church, but special-interest small groups already exist also. Why not capitalize on this special interest? People are doing things together. Wouldn't it be wonderful if the church could capture the energy that is generated in this fashion and put it to work for Jesus? This will be discussed in the next chapter.

5
New Doors for the Small Church

How many doors are there in your church? We are not talking about the front door and the back door or a fire exit. We mean: How many ways are available for people to get into the church where you serve? One reason many churches do not grow is that people can't find a way to get in. They would like to get in, and some have even tried. But they have found it impossible. And tragically, some who have tried have been disappointed when they did make the approach.

I am going to say something that will sound unkind. But it is, sadly, very true. *The average small church is not a friendly church.* Oh, they say they are, and I suppose that they think they are; but they are not. They are friendly with each other. People who have known each other for years meet and greet with warm handshakes and fond embraces. But the visitors—well, that is another matter! Now the real tragedy here is this: Because they are friendly with old friends, they go joyfully along thinking they have a friendly church, when all the while they treat strangers as if they were icebergs. The average small church is not a very friendly place to visit. That is one reason why they are small.

Since visitors are not likely to tell the pastor and members that their church is unfriendly, it is not easy to discover this fact. Perhaps one indication might be that they do not return. That should tell us something. When people visit once and do not return, there has to be *some* reason. It is a known fact that most people begin attending a church because their friends bring them with them. The percentage given is usually about 34 percent. Maybe the friends they go with for the first time help them break the ice. At any rate, the greatest single reason for people attending church is that they are brought along by friends. That much we can be certain about.

If I had any question about my church being friendly, I would get someone that none of them knew, perhaps from another city, to come for the express reason of testing my congregation. If the report was unfavorable, I would surely use this bit of information to change matters.

Once inside the church, it is still possible for visitors to discover that they are not really in at all. They just thought they got in. They are still outsiders. And some churches can surely make people feel like outsiders! In some instances it takes years for people to actually reach the place where they are accepted by the church. Some people never make the grade. That little power structure can keep the door closed so tightly that a person would have to be born into the church to get in.

One church well known to the writer had a lady who made the decision as to who would get in and who would be branded as an eternal visitor. She was, I suppose, a good woman. She was a hard worker and did an excellent job with every assignment—that is, if she chose to take the assignment. But she had the power to keep people off the church board; she controlled the music; she controlled the finances; in short, that lady was the "head honcho." That church lost many fine families because they could not pass her little test. The test was simple—recognizing her as the controlling force. Whether she meant to be that way or didn't even realize the damage she caused, that was nevertheless the situation.

Let's Create Some New Church Doors

Most small churches have but one door. It is the Sunday School. We go out week after week and try to get people to come to Sunday School. We have contests to get people to "come and be counted." That always seemed like a low motive to me. But that is what we do; and that is just about *all* most churches are doing.

Now there is nothing wrong with getting people to come to Sunday School and, hopefully, staying for the morning service. That is a door into the church. If they get in, I suppose it doesn't matter in the end how they get in. But there are a lot of people who will not get in by this method. There are a lot of people who do not like Sunday School. In fact, there are people who just don't like any kind of school. They hated school when they had to go. Once out of public school they vowed they would never go to school again. What about them? What about the people who have a limited education? What about people who are poor readers and fear being called on to read? What about the man who is just not comfortable in a classroom situation? What about all of these people? Are we just going to forget them? If the Sunday School is the only door into our churches, we are greatly limiting the size of our churches. But worse, we are closing the door to the kingdom of God for a lot of people.

Revivals were at one time a major door into the church. Perhaps they still are in some instances. Sometimes people come to a revival and are converted without previously having been identified with the church through the Sunday School or some other outreach effort. But this is not typical. Revivals are still one of the major doors into the kingdom of God. But we are not talking about conversion at this point. We are talking about the door into the church, the door into the fellowship and acceptance by the people of the church. Conversion can and should occur by exposure to the ministry of the church. This might be during a revival or in a regular Sunday service. When and how a person is saved is not as important as the fact that he is saved. But revivals today are usually the second phase of the conversion process, after the people first start attending the church services. As such they are not the door.

LET'S FIND THE DOOR

It is important that the church leaders understand the necessity of making every project a door for people to enter the fellowship of the congregation. Unless they see what is being done, they may hinder rather than help the process. When new avenues of approach are developing, the leadership needs to keep these free from obstruction insofar as possible.

The familiar door of the Sunday School with its efforts to bring in new class members should be continued. This is a time-tested and dependable method. In the same sense, every other group should serve the same purpose. Missionary societies and chapters, youth groups already in existence, every organized small group should be an arm of evangelism. But why need churches be limited to these? As many more as can be found should be used.

New and exciting ideas can be generated. If leaders can get people excited about something new, a new source of power has been unleashed. New things do generate excitement. They also represent a new area of ministry to better serve the people of the church. We have found some helpful doors that have made it easier for people to enter our church.

We have developed what we have chosen to call the S.E.E.D. Hour (Sunday Evening Educational Development). This is conducted on Sunday night at 6:00. It is an adult study session. This time is wasted in so many churches. While the teens and juniors meet, the adults have nothing to do. We have a very well attended study session. We study what we feel is most needed. We spent one year on church growth back before it became the talk of the church. This was very helpful. It is done with open discussion and whatever materials the teacher may choose to introduce. We use an overhead projector, filmstrips, films, posters, and anything else we can think of with which to teach. It is open-ended with no planned finishing date.

We move from one subject to another as interest and need dictate. Sometimes the teacher and the pastor make the choice. Sometimes the interest of the group makes the choice evident. But attendance and interest has not flagged over several years. We have had studies in personal finance and budgeting. We have had Bible studies and CST courses. There is available on the market today an abundance of material that is perfectly suited for this kind of study.

On Sunday night at our church it looks much like Sunday School on Sunday morning. The teens are studying with some taped material by Dr. James Dobson; the juniors are meeting; Bible Quiz groups meet; the nursery is in full operation; the young adults are into a Bible study; and everyone is deeply involved in something worthwhile. Maybe this is why the Sunday night attendance looks more like a Sunday morning crowd!

Wednesday night is much the same way. The Caravan groups meet on this night. We have, from time to time, special study groups that meet separately from the regular prayer meeting. After prayer meeting the adult choir meets for its practice. Prayer meeting attendance is now larger than the Sunday School attendance was just four years ago.

On Sunday morning while the worship service is in progress, the children's church is also meeting. The director of the junior choir, after the song service with the adults, meets with them for their practice. A lot of double-heading becomes necessary as the church program grows. This is especially true when there is not a lot of paid assistance.

We have stated all of this to show how the ministry of a church can be greatly multiplied and how that multiplication can make the church grow. Not only will the church grow, but it will become much more effective in terms of quality ministry.

When I came to this church as pastor, the record Sunday School attendance was 189. We used to have a rally day with increased attendance, and we had bedlam with a big increase in attendance. Today we are averaging well beyond what just a few years ago was a record attendance, and the operation is smooth and quiet. The secret of the moderate flow is organization. A well-planned and well-organized church is far more efficient, not to mention being more enjoyable to operate or attend. If everyone knows what his job is and how to do it, he is far more likely to do his job with faithfulness than with a hit-or-miss program where no one knows for sure just what is supposed to happen, or what is happening.

Now, so far, we are still on square one concerning people who have reservations about study groups. For a person so inhibited, whether it is Sunday School on Sunday morning or something on Sunday night that looks very much like Sunday School, we still have the same problem. If a man doesn't like school, night school is still school to him. So we must find another way to reach him.

6
Doors That Are Open All Week

Some of the saddest sights around are the thousands of churches sitting dark and empty almost every night and equally inactive all day. Sunday is a busy day with most churches. Many have a Wednesday night prayer meeting, where a minority of the members gather for an hour or two. Maybe there will be an occasional revival or some other special activity. But think how many hours the church is completely deserted. Dark by night and deserted by day—what a sad testimony to the community where it is located.

It is little wonder that some theologians a few years back came up with the "God is dead" idea. If we look at the church buildings, we have one area where they could get their idea. Every week has 168 hours in it. The church has something going on about 8 hours of this time. On Sunday morning there is 1 hour for Sunday School and another for church. Sunday night could account for another 2 hours. Wednesday night the church will probably have a prayer meeting and perhaps a choir practice after that. Some little part of the church possibly will be used for board meetings or class meetings or some social activity. Many small churches do not even have this much activity. But 160 hours of each week the church is virtually vacant and empty.

When the cost of the average church building is considered, this can only be interpreted as a tragic waste of God's money. If that is all we are going to use these expensive facilities, we are forced to face some serious questions. The average small church built in the last 10 years probably cost well over $100,000; many cost far more. But even when the minimum figure is allowed, do we have the right to spend that much money on an almost perpetually empty building? Is that all God expects us to do with the lovely building He has helped us to build? Is it really to the glory of God to erect such monuments of darkness and silence? Is there a better way to utilize what represents a fantastic commitment of God's resources?

Not only do I believe there is a better way, but I believe we are bound by every law of good stewardship to find this way. The church, if it is alive, must be alive all the time. We do not need a weekly resurrection on Sunday morning and then a death Sunday night with the church slumbering in the tomb all week. The New Testament Church added to its ranks daily. And they didn't even have a building. We have covered this nation with lovely edifices of masonry and mortar and wood. We have a hard time adding to our ranks any of the time. I really don't think that is the way God wants it to be.

Let's Put the Church to Work All Week

Granted, we will not likely use the sanctuary every night in the week. Though it might be ideal to make better use of it, the high cost of utilities would be a mitigating factor. But there are other ways to keep the church active.

Larger churches usually have a secretary working in the church office during the day. She is answering the phone, writing letters, and taking care of the normal office responsibilities. But as any businessman who does business with the small church will tell you, the small church usually does not have anyone around much during business hours when deliveries are made and service of equipment is expected. The pastor is frequently in and out of the church building. But he is usually out when he needs to be in and in when he needs to be out. The members think he doesn't visit enough—that is, unless they happen to call the church. Then they can't understand where he is all the time. Why is he never on the job like other people?

In the preceding chapter we talked about the doors that are open on Sunday that give access into the fellowship of the church. We can also open doors into the fellowship of the church and create an ongoing, living church that operates seven days a week, or nearly so.

CIRCLES OF CONCERN

Pastor Millard Reed, who is minister of First Church of the Nazarene in Nashville, has written a little book entitled *Let Your Church Grow.* In it are details on how to organize the "Circles of Concern." I will not repeat them here. But we did what the book suggested. We have in our church 11 circles with 8 or 10 families in each circle. The 105 families that make up the fellowship of our church have all been assigned to a circle. Not all of these people are active. Some are church members, some are Sunday School members, but others are people who only come occasionally. But all of them have some identification with our church. If you were to ask any of them, they would name our church as their church. If death came, they would look to our church for support and comfort. Their children will have their weddings in our church. We claim them and they claim us. These so-called fringe people are very important to any church.

Each circle has a leader who gives supervision to his circle. This involves not only spiritual consideration but every other need as well. If they become less regular at church, the circle leader will contact them. If there is a death or sickness or unemployment, the circle leader is there to help. The other members of the circle are informed. If the need is beyond their ability to help, the pastor brings other circles into the picture. But in most instances the circle can take care of its own. The circles have occasional times of fellowship. Once in a while at prayer meeting we have the entire prayer meeting group divide up into circles and have small prayer groups all over the church.

There is also endless variety to the way the Circles of Concern can be used to further the spiritual life of the church and enhance the fellowship of the church. Many people will feel more comfortable in these small groups. They are a little family in the church. In our church they are divided geographically rather than socially or by age, so this would hopefully help to avoid the problem of cliques forming among them. It also produces a cross section of the fellowship, since Sunday School classes and other small groups are more or less a division by special interests because of age grouping. These people live near each other and do have that in common.

Here is another door into the church. Lonely shut-ins, sick people, unchurched people, and others can be found by the circles and immediately placed in the circle. The pastor then publishes their name in the weekly newsletter and puts them on the mailing list. The only requirement for membership is that they feel their need of God and His people. But from then on they are on the prayer list and the visitation list. They have a church and pastor to turn to in time of need.

SOCIAL COMMITTEES

We came up with this idea a number of years ago. It has proven to be of great assistance in many ways. Every church has social responsibilities. There are showers for weddings and expectant mothers. There are other equally necessary social demands. We found a simple way to meet these demands and at the same time involve people in another small group.

Every lady is placed in one of three Social Committees. (We have at times had four, but presently three seems to be sufficient.) A group leader and an assistant is selected with great care. These have to be real leaders. Those on the committee serving with them are also selected with care. Each group has some of the more active and some of the less active ladies of the church.

As occasions arise for responsibility, they take turns preparing showers or similar duties. Not only does this relieve the faithful few from having to do all the entertaining, but it involves many more ladies in the operation of the church. In churches such as ours where many baby showers are necessary, this is a very helpful arrangement. The leader calls her committee members, and together they take care of the whole occasion when their turn comes. Everyone is invited to the shower, but the committee takes care of refreshments, decorations, games, or whatever is expected at such gatherings.

Each committee is a small group with people working together as a group. They enjoy the fellowship of the occasion without feeling lost in the crowd. Many times ladies who otherwise would never get involved in the operation of the church find meaningful opportunities for service even in this limited way.

When a large gathering is planned, such as an all-church dinner, the committee leaders with their assistants (six in all) meet as an executive committee and organize the combined committees to meet the demands of the larger responsibility.

Varied Other Weekday Activities

The possibilities for other weekday activities that will bring others to church are without limit. Most churches will discover things that interest their people. Certainly the church will want to meet the need of their people and at the same time remember the cause for the existence of the church in its redemptive mission.

Many churches have an athletic program. While this is usually seasonal, it can be made very attractive in bringing unsaved people into the church fellowship. Many men will come first to a ball game, make friends with other men, and then come to a Sunday School class. Wives who have a hard time getting their husbands to church can use this method very effectively if the church will provide this door for them to enter. A variety of other possibilities are on the drawing board, so to speak, with our church. We will explore and test some of them in the coming year.

A "Piddler's Class" has been suggested. This is a group who get together to sew or paint or share some other hobby with the group in a Christian environment. The art class would include some instruction from someone in the church who can paint. All of these would be low-key and informal. It would be just for those who would like to come.

What about a baby-sitting service one night a week for young couples who need an evening for shopping or just dinner together alone away from the children? Many young couples can't afford a baby-sitter but desperately need to go out together for a "date." This could mean a lot to their marriage and home. The church could offer this to its people and make a lot of friends at the same time. And it probably would cost the church very little, if anything. If some of the older ladies would really get this on their hearts as a method of soul winning, who can say how much good would come of it?

All of these things bring life to the church. These are opportunities to use that big, empty church for the glory of God and the good of God's people. Some part of the building should be lighted and in service every night.

The primary mission of the church is to bring men and women to the Lord Jesus Christ. It does not matter, in the end, what we are doing if we are not saving the lost. But it is unlikely that the church can run a continuous revival. That is, mass evangelism, which is about all most churches do to win people to Christ, cannot be conducted every night. Yet, the New Testament Church was winning people daily. They must have had something going all the time. That "something" will be the continuation of this discussion in the next chapter.

7

Laymen Winning the Lost

When I first heard of the method of presenting the gospel to someone in his home and actually giving an altar call, I thought it sounded like a grand idea. I have seen many people saved in their homes and other unlikely places across the years of my ministry. But it was usually a matter of finding someone under deep conviction for sin and helping him find the Savior then and there. Many times I have had people call me on the phone and ask me to come pray with them or some member of their family. That was not new. But what was new was going into a home with plans to preach a little sermon to one person and then ask him to then and there kneel by the coffee table and repent. What was even more revolutionary was training laymen to do this.

All of this sounded like an excellent idea. If I could have a big group of people from our church going out winning people to Christ, it would be the most fantastic thing I could think of to build God's kingdom.

I knew I could never get others to do what I could not or would not do. I read all the books I could find, studied the manuals, and listened to the tapes. I was determined to learn. There was no one to teach me—no on-the-job training sessions were available. Then after I felt somewhat prepared, I made my plans to go and win someone to Christ. I prayed for the Lord to give a family for Jesus on the *first try* if this was His will for my ministry. Maybe that was not a wise prayer. But that is the way I prayed.

There was a man and his wife who had attended our church several times over a three-month period. They were in their mid-40s; a nice middle-class couple. I chose them. I followed the plan just as the books said. Their response was also just as the book said. The man, to whom I addressed most of my comments, offered the classic answers: "I always treat people right; I live by the golden rule"—it sounded as if he had read the book too!

Then I came to the altar call: "Jesus said, 'Behold, I stand at the door . . .' " I asked, "Wouldn't you like to open that door and invite Him in?"

His wife, sitting unnoticed for the moment, responded, "I would!" The man followed his wife in kneeling then and there, and both gave their hearts to Christ. All three of us were overjoyed. I went home thrilled and happy that I had "found the way." I now was determined to present the plan to the church, train a big group, and send them out to follow the example of their pastor.

THE GREAT IDEA THAT DIDN'T WORK

When Sunday came, I was ready with a sermon on

soul winning. I preached it with all of the excitement that my past experience afforded. Then I launched the plan. I had about five women who took the course and learned the material. But somehow they just never seemed to get excited about the grand plan. We had two or three who did win someone to the Lord, but it was far from the glorious avalanche of soul winning that I had envisioned. I was able to win a number of people by this method, but not very many of them ever came to our church. Not that they had to come to our church to make it to heaven, but it would have been encouraging if some of them had.

Second opportunities do come. In my next church I used what I had learned; I used films; I really put some gusto into the promotion of personal soul winning. By this time I had won, personally, quite a number of people to Christ by this method. Now I was preaching with some authority and a lot of experience. The people sat there and listened to my sermons on why they should win souls with that little "Mona Lisa smile" on their faces. Some even ventured a weak amen. And that was it.

The Cause Is Not Lost

Now I can give a list of about 50 ways that won't work. I tried them all with equal success—none. I knew that some churches have fabulous soul-winning teams—or so they report. But I never did get a great number of people sufficiently motivated to be able to make such claims. Yet, we do have a successful soul-winning effort working in our church. No one is interested in ways that do not work. But I offer below some of the things that I learned over a 10-year period that will work.

1. The pastor must himself be a personal soul winner. If the pastor cannot or will not go out and win people in their homes, he will never be able to get others to do so. I have seen people converted in the hospital, in automobiles, in homes, and in about every other place where it is possible to talk with them about Christ. For many years this has been a way of life with me.

2. Find *one man* (or woman) and develop that person. Teach just one person at a time to win souls. It is essential to take that one out with you and demonstrate how it is done.

3. This person then becomes a trainer to teach another to do likewise. This takes a lot of time but it will work. In fact, I personally believe it is the only way that will work. I have never been able to get a sizeable group to do anything other than listen. They never get around to winning anyone to the Lord. But, by working with one at a time, it can be done.

4. "Until it becomes an obsession, it will always be a dream." I don't know who first said that, but I know that it is true. When the pastor becomes so obsessed with the idea that he will not take failure as an option, he will make it work. But not until then!

5. Make up your mind that it will be slow, demanding, and sometimes disappointing work. It demands real commitment. It is not a cure-all. It may not do much to increase your Sunday School attendance.

6. It is not as exciting as mass evangelism. You will be talking to one or two people at the most. Frequently you will fail. Sometimes, when you do succeed in leading them to Christ, you will never see them again. There is no great drama in most instances. No one will see you "perform" as the great soul winner.

7. A lay-witnessing program (or whatever you choose to call it), while it is a vital area for growth, will not by itself ever guarantee a great church. It is always done in conjunction with other programs operating in the church. It is a tool. You need a good church to invite people to after you have won them to Christ. It works well with a bussing program. It is very useful with a day-care center or kindergarten. It gives you a method to reach many people that you will never be able to preach to from the pulpit.

THE COMPROMISE

Not everybody has the gift of evangelism. In fact, I have abandoned the word *evangelism* almost entirely where laypeople are concerned. It frightens them; all they can think of is a powerful evangelist in the pulpit. Lay witnessing is a little easier for nonprofessionals to accept. Peter Wagner suggests that the gift of evangelism is indeed a gift of the Spirit limited to a minority in any church. He suggests 10 percent as a realistic expectation for the membership. Perhaps he is right. We can only hope that in churches of 100 members they can find 10 real soul winners to join their pastor in reaching the lost.

Our present method is working quite well. We call our group our SWAT team. This is short for Soul Winning And Testifying. But the acronym SWAT also carries with it another concept. We pick out one person, zero in on him, and stay with it until we get him converted. The team will pray and fast for that individual until something happens in that life. We are presently involved in another training and reorganizational period. This time we have made no public announcement either from the pulpit or in print. We selected several people who we felt had the gifts and commitment and privately invited them to the session which is meeting on Wednesday night during prayer meeting. They also meet at other times when they go into the homes. When these five are trained, then others will be invited. But very little is said about the whole program. That way we get the right people without hurting the feelings of others.

THE OBJECTIONS THAT AROSE

That anyone would object to winning people to Christ came as quite a shock to me. I thought that was what we were all trying to do. But most of the objections came because of either abuse or misuse. Others just didn't understand the method. I personally have never found it helpful to just go door to door presenting the gospel. Others have had a fair amount of success with this "cold turkey" approach. But for me it is best if I have some previous contact. Usually the people have attended our church. I won a lovely couple who are in their retirement years. They have been attending our church faithfully since. They are growing in the Lord daily. But they started attending church before I presented the gospel to them. The lady had even been to the altar. But she was finally converted in the home, as was her husband. Their conversion is very real to them. They both have a good testimony.

Some have seen this method as a threat to revivals. Never! Revivals are essential to the life of our church. We call a good evangelist twice a year and conduct a full revival. This is usually in addition to weekend revivals. Churches that have had little success in revivals will probably have even less success with this method, because it is much harder. If they have failed in the one case, they will fail in the other. Their problems are not methods but determination.

Facing the Hard, Cold Facts

The hard, cold facts are these: Some people will never be won to Christ unless we use methods other than those that have repeatedly been failing. What are we going to do when people will not respond to the public altar call? Will we let them be lost? What about people who will not come to our revivals? Will we let them be lost? I believe that if we really care about the unsaved as we say we do, we will do everything we can to get them saved. If a man has fallen into the water and is going under, who cares how we get him out of his situation? The important thing is saving the man. If someone comes along who has an unfamiliar method that gets the man out of the water, who cares? The drowning man certainly does not care.

There is a fringe benefit to this matter of laymen winning people to Christ. It is what it does for them. The blessing they get and the overflow they spread throughout the church will be worth all the effort. It only takes one testimony from some little, quiet housewife about how she led her neighbor to Christ the day before to have a dramatic effect on the Wednesday night prayer meeting. Then if you take that person into the church with this little lady who won her standing by her side, you will have something going in your church that will make it all worthwhile. You will forget the long, disappointing hours of failure when it seemed that nothing was going to happen. And you will wonder why you didn't try sooner and work harder.

8

Making Disciples
Who Make Disciples

We come now to one of the most critical issues in the present-day small church. Certainly it is the biggest cause for that church remaining small year after year. If we have one failure that is greater than any other, it is in the matter of making disciples out of church members. What we find in many churches can best be described as a congregation of spectators. Why have we not concentrated on making disciples? Why have we not taught people to do something? Or know something? Was it not God's plan that the laymen run the church in its day-to-day function? What we have in the average small church is a situation where the pastor actually runs the church while the laymen sit around and watch him do his thing.

In many churches the average layman couldn't carry on the church if he had a chance. In most churches he doesn't get that chance. But if he did, he would not have the vaguest idea of the most elementary things. There may be a few key people who can do some things, but not the average man in the pew.

Shortly after arriving at one church that I served as pastor, I planned a baptismal service. The church building was quite old but attractive and reasonably well built for its day. The baptistry was somewhat of a mystery. There were some pipes, but I could find no way to turn on the water. There was not one person in that church who could help me, even though they had been worshipping there for many years and had had many baptismal services. I had to make a long-distance phone call to the former pastor to find out how the baptistry worked.

Some months later we had another problem. When we had extremely heavy rain over an extended period of time, the parsonage basement would begin to fill with water. When it started, it really came in. In fact, when I discovered this predicament, it was already about a foot deep. Once again I could not discover how to turn on the pump that had been installed for this recurring event. The pump worked, as I discovered, not by electricity but water pressure. This, I suppose, made it useful even during a power failure. But how could we get the thing to operate? While the basement rapidly filled with water, I called every board member and some who were not on the church board. Not one person even knew that the parsonage had a sump pump, much less how it worked. Again I called the former pastor.

Now these church members were intelligent people who successfully worked at a variety of jobs and made a good living. Some even had their own businesses. How is it that they were so ignorant about the church? They had never been taught one thing about the building in which they worshipped. Sad to say, this is not an exceptional case. This is typical of many small churches. The pastor just goes ahead and does everything and never takes time to teach the people one thing about the church and its day-to-day operation.

These are practical things and seemingly not all that important. But when you begin to multiply them by the scores of similar necessities of daily living, it begins to take on huge proportions. And when you remember that what is being said here reflects a basic philosophy, you begin to realize that it is indeed a sizeable threat to progress.

The Bible has a lot more to say about these matters than we have given evidence of by our preaching. Two significant verses of scripture come to mind. First, 2 Tim. 2:2 exhorts, "And the things that thou hast heard of me among many witnesses, the same commit thou to faithful men, who shall be able to teach others also." Why are we not doing this? Why have we not taught laymen to teach other laymen to carry on the work of God? I know, we have Sunday School and call that teaching each other. But who ever heard of a Sunday School class that ever taught anybody how to operate the baptistry? Or, for that matter, the pump in the basement of the parsonage? These are the things that the pastor needs help with. Now you can translate that into a hundred other things around the church. The point is, these things are the layman's job. If the sons of Levi leave all of this to the priest, we don't even need his tribe.

The second verse is even more condemning. Matt. 28:19 is a very familiar scripture. Possibly every preacher has preached from it, and every layman has heard more than one sermon from it. But there is a word we have been missing because of the weak translation in the King James version. It reads, "Go ye therefore, and *teach* all nations . . ." The word "teach" there is translated "disciple" in almost every modern translation, and even in the KJV it is rendered so in the margin. But we have missed the importance of this truth in a rather consistent pattern.

Unless we do more than teach our people, we will never really fulfill the Great Commission. *We must make disciples out of them.* Any pastor of a small church who has taken the time to read this far has already said to himself (and probably to his wife), "Yeah, that is all well and fine. If you have people in the church who are capable of really doing these things, anyone can make the church succeed. But where can I find these kinds of laypeople?"

A pastor friend of mine was discussing these matters with a pastor from another denomination that is famous for large churches. This man, himself the pastor of a big congregation, frankly told him, "The trouble with you people is that you don't trust your laymen."

This is no doubt a major problem in many chronically small churches. The pastor just does not trust his laypeople. He actually thinks they can't do anything. He feels that he has to do it all or it won't get done. Or, at best, it will not be done right. He is either afraid to really turn leadership over to laypeople, or—and this is even worse—he is afraid they will do it better than he can and show up his own weaknesses. It takes a big man to admit that there are people in his church who are more capable than he is. But this is frequently the case. And they are just begging for the opportunity to use their gifts and talents for the glory of God and the building of the Kingdom.

In the next chapter we will discuss the training of people for quality service for God. It can and must be done. The alternative is slow death in the small church. We bury too many churches every year. That mortality rate will only increase as competition with efficient churches increases. And increase it will. The TV churches are putting pressure on the small church. Our people see these giant organizations and wonder why we are doing so poorly. Some are slipping away to larger churches with more to offer while, year after year, the little church plugs along with the same little congregation which is getting smaller and smaller.

Before we move to the matter of how to develop disciples in the small church, I would like to call attention to another important matter.

MOTIVATION

Down in our hearts we all know something that we are not talking much about. I have attended a number of church growth seminars and similar workshops. Some of these have been national in scope and presented world-famous speakers. I have read many books on church growth and evangelism and soul winning. But I have heard little or nothing about something, the lack of which is so basic as a cause for failure: that is, we must be motivated before we can motivate others. If we are not turned on, we will never make it happen to others. The reason many churches are stuck on dead center is because the pastors are stuck in that same spot. We will never make disciples out of bench-warming church members until we get excited about it.

This is one thing that cannot be faked. Just jumping around and shouting a lot will not do it. The people will be able to tell that it is all for show. But if deep in our hearts there is a real fire burning, its warmth will be felt by others. Soon the cold chill will vanish from our churches. Things will begin to move ahead. If we stoke the furnace with a steady hand, we will eventually build up some real steam in the old boiler.

One of my members gave me some cassette tapes. I carried them along to listen to as I drove on a trip. It was a bad, stormy night. The rain was falling and lightning flashed frequently as we drove along the freeway. But I didn't pay much attention. I was so captivated by what the speaker was saying, I could hardly keep my mind on driving. The audience he was speaking to must have been quite large. They were very responsive to what they were hearing also. He was speaking about being free. He told how excited he was about this new freedom. His friends had decorated his little Toyota truck with flags. He told how he rushed into the house when he got home; how he grabbed his wife and swung her around; he told how he ran out on the back porch. He had me so excited I was wishing I could get him to come to hold a revival in our church.

When I came to myself at the end of the tape, I had to remind myself he wasn't preaching. He was not a preacher, nor was he even talking about religion. He was selling soap. He was telling how he became a millionaire with this company, selling their products. But he had me so excited that I was ready to stop at the nearest phone booth and get him to sign me up.

Then I thought: If he could get that excited about what he was doing, how in the world can we be so mundane about what we are doing? There is nothing wrong with selling soap. Maybe his ideas were good. Maybe they would work. I have been in some church services that were so dead and dry that I would not want any of it even if they paid me to take it. Then we wonder why we have a hard time getting unsaved people interested. The big surprise to me is that they even come at all, much less join us.

This man on the tape was a success because he was excited about what he was doing. Maybe this is not the way things ought to be, but it is the way things are. If you can't get excited about what you are trying to do, you might just as well give up. For one thing is certain: No one else will ever get excited about it if you are not. The success of many religious groups is not in their doctrinal accuracy or theological soundness. Their success lies wholly in the fact that they are so excited about what they are doing that people just can't resist believing they have found the way.

If error can live on the excitement of its advocate, I don't believe excitement would hurt truth. All growing churches, large and small, have pastors and people that are excited about what they are doing. They have leadership that is highly motivated. That motivation excites people. They come to church because they feel something among the membership that is attractive. They feel something that is thrilling. Maybe they cannot define it, but they know it is there.

And the other side of the coin is unfortunately true: They know when it is not there.

9

Making Disciples Who Will Make a Church

It is with some reluctance that an attempt is made to write a chapter on how to make disciples. Situations and people are so different. Things that work in one place will not be helpful at all in another. Perhaps it will be most helpful to just tell the story of our church at this point.

Our church is far from perfect. There are so many things that we come up short in. No doubt others could do more in the realm of making disciples than we are doing. But we have had some success. We are growing at a rate that seems healthy. We are winning new people to Christ. If what we have done will be helpful to others, we hope they will use it.

The Importance of the Building Blocks

A good building cannot be built with poor building materials. If we want quality, then we must build with quality materials. While this is a self-evident truth, some people do not seem to believe it. We must start with the individual, for churches are made up of individual people. Even if there are 1,000 people in a church, they are all separate ànd distinct personalities. We must treat them as such and work with them as such.

Attention must be given to developing quality disciples. This means that church membership must lead to discipleship. Everybody must have a job for which he or she is trained and qualified. What develops in almost every small church is a pastor-centered church rather than one that is people centered. When a local church changes its modus operandi to become more people oriented, this does not mean that the pastor is not an important factor in the church. It does not mean that he is not giving strong leadership to the church. It in no way tarnishes his image as pastor.

What being people-centered does mean is that the people feel important also. They are part of the real church. They are in on the planning. They are recognized as intelligent human beings with the ability to contribute more than their tithe. They are challenged to develop their abilities to contribute to their church in a vital and meaningful way. When people begin to see themselves as important parts of the operation of the church, they will try harder to be better disciples. They will study and read. They will also have more cause to rejoice over the victories won. And, above all, they will feel more responsible for the success of the church.

EDUCATING THE DISCIPLES

How then can we train our church members to

become disciples? We have found some very helpful tools.

Communication is vital. We can never take it for granted that everyone knows what is happening in the church. This is especially true of a growing church. We have found it absolutely essential to have these things in our church.

If there is not one already, the church should get a good mimeograph machine. This is not an area in which to skimp, but rather to get a machine that will produce quality printing. So many small churches have the poorest equipment. Some have none whatever. Sometimes it is better to take the copy to a nearby printer who will run it on his machine. It is preferable for the church to have its own equipment in order to be able to run material when printers are closed or on a moment's notice. With a good machine this can be done in a matter of minutes.

We publish a weekly newsletter. It is difficult to see how any church can operate without this means of communication. In this we put everything we are doing. *It is people centered.* A spot check of one issue recently revealed that it contained the names of over 50 people. Who is sick, who had a baby, who is away on a trip; these things about people make it interesting and readable. The program of the church and what classes and groups are doing is also there. The attendance for the past week is there (even when it is not so good). This newsletter is published every Tuesday. People look forward to its arrival at a regular time each week.

Several other means of communication have also been found to be vital. For one thing we have found it essential to give everyone in leadership a box in the church office. The pastor has a box. Sunday School teachers, department heads, and group leaders all have a box. If they want to get a message to the pastor, they just put a note in my box. They do likewise for each other. Material to go in the newsletter is just dropped in the box designated for this purpose. It is almost impossible to get around to seeing everyone we need to talk to on Sunday morning. Sometimes I do not even see some people at church. They are in their Sunday School department while I am in mine. They may be working in the children's church or the nursery during the worship hour. I seldom get to speak to them at church. But the box will allow us to get a message to each other when it is necessary.

We have found it helpful to publish a monthly calendar. Stencils are available to mimeograph them on. We print a Sunday morning church bulletin. The monthly calendar is inserted in this. Together they keep everyone aware of the activities both weekly and monthly.

THE CHURCH DIRECTORY

Another thing we have found absolutely essential is a church directory. This is printed twice a year. It contains a total listing of every position in the church together with names, addresses, and phone numbers.

We list the name of every family connected with the church along with children's names. It looks like this:

SMITH   242-2121
John, Mary, Sue, Terri
1034 Main Street

We try to include every item of information about the church organization and its leadership. These directories are distributed to every family. This becomes a vital tool in communication, education, and even in prayer. It helps to tie the whole church together and reminds people of the whole program. New people coming in have immediately available to them a total picture of the church and its operation. Our directories are usually about 15 pages in size. We print them on colored paper and try to make them as attractive as we can. We include a few pictures to give them eye appeal. These can be drawn right on the mimeograph stencil with a stylus. The whole thing is not very expensive and becomes priceless. It will prove to be helpful in so many ways throughout every phase of the church operation.

Once we have the ability to really communicate with our people, we can begin training them in so many ways. So much is available today that we did not have in years that are gone. When I started preaching, we had to more or less improvise with the few things we did have. Today the supply seems endless. And new methods and materials are constantly being introduced. Films, cassette tapes, study books, and filmstrips are all available and affordable to any church.

One source that is frequently missed is the public library. Almost any city today has a library, and the material is usually free. One can not only get film and filmstrips, but the libraries usually have projectors that are available to churches. They can be checked out just as a book. The first thing I do after my furniture is unloaded at a new church is to go join the public library. And I make use of the library card, too. Any church, no matter how small or poor, can provide valuable training for their congregation in this manner. Too few pastors take advantage of this opportunity.

Every church should have a training program directed by the most capable person available. This will require the building of a church library which should be an ongoing thing. Most of the books needed are available in paperback editions and are affordable. These can be purchased a few at a time. The director of Christian Service Training can not only keep up with the books but also the courses completed by the individuals. This can become an exciting thing. Certificates and diplomas should be awarded publicly in the morning worship service. The pastor should take advantage of this to encourage others to train themselves for service. The director should be a person who will encourage people on a one-to-one basis to study the material available. The director will also be able to give guidance as to what the student should study to prepare for his particular need and interest.

THE GIFTS OF THE SPIRIT

Recently we had a churchwide emphasis on the gifts of the Spirit. I preached six sermons on the subject. We encouraged everyone to find and develop his personal gift. It was thrilling to see some who had been on the sidelines move into the mainstream of church life. We had people signing up for things for which they were willing to assume responsibility.

Printed forms were made available for those who were willing to state their feeling about what God had for them to do. It came as a revelation to some that there were so many things that had to be done to keep the church in operation. There came an awakening to others who had been spiritual Rip Van Winkles all of their Christian lives.

When opportunities are created for Christians to fulfill the gifts of the Spirit and proper emphasis is brought to bear on the subject, things begin to happen. To tell people they have a gift and then not provide an opportunity to use it can do as much harm as good. To preach to people about the needs of the church without providing them with proper training about the gifts God has given them to meet these needs is useless. Why not put the two together as God intended?

THE CONSOLATION

I walked down the hall of our annex one Sunday night. In every adult room I saw people studying the

Word of God. The teens were in another department studying with the use of tapes prepared by Dr. James Dobson. The senior adults were studying a course on the second coming of Christ. The juniors were preparing for a District Bible Quiz Meet. Everywhere people were studying something. Soon the group would assemble for the Sunday evening service. There was excitement about the Bible in the very atmosphere of the church. And this is not an exceptional Sunday. This is typical of Sunday and Wednesday nights. We begin church on Sunday night at five o'clock with our teen choir practice, Bible Quiz groups meeting, and usually several other groups meeting here and there. We usually do not turn out the lights until about ten o'clock. We all go home very much aware that we have been to church Sunday night.

Most churches that have trouble getting people to attend their Sunday night services probably are not giving very much of an incentive for attending. People will still attend Sunday night services if they feel it is worth their time. But if the Sunday night service is just a repeat of the morning worship with two-thirds of the congregation absent, it is little wonder the two-thirds are absent.

10

Using the Organization
in the Small Church

One day, so the old story goes, a man was out in a clover field, killing bees. He was using a flyswatter, killing them one at a time. He would go here and there, swatting one after another. But near the edge of the field there was a tree growing. So he worked his way over to the tree. As he got nearer the tree, he saw a big, gray ball hanging from one of the lower limbs. Down near the bottom of this thing, he saw several of his prey crawling around close to what looked like a hole. He rushed over and gave them one big swat.

Several days later in the hospital a friend was visiting him. "What happened, Bill?" the friend inquired. Bill told him the story of his efforts with the flyswatter on a one-by-one basis.

"Then I met this bunch that was organized," Bill continued.

Organization does make a difference. The reason some small churches fail is that they do not utilize their own potential. One of the great general superintendents in the Church of the Nazarene used to tell the pastors, "Fellows, you are not overworked—you are underorganized." Probably he was right. Some people work themselves to death doing the same job others do with ease. The difference is organization.

Now it is possible to have such an organization that we are worked to death keeping the thing going. Several years ago the newspapers carried the story of the man who lived near the city dump. He had over a number of years collected items discarded by the citizens of the city. With a little help from a few junkyard rejects, he constructed a huge machine that ran perfectly. It was very complex. It used several sources of power, including steam, batteries, and a small engine. He had it on display for the general public to see and admire. Everyone was amazed until someone asked the question, "What does it do?"

"Do? It runs!" the man exclaimed.

"But does it make anything?" the inquirer persisted.

"Well, not really," the inventor had to admit.

Some organizations just keep themselves going, and that is about all they can boast. Unfortunately some churches are about the same way. The only claim they can make is that they keep themselves going. A few are not even doing that.

During one prayer meeting we were studying from the fifth chapter of the Acts. We came to the 28th verse that reads "Behold, ye have filled Jerusalem with your doctrine." We discussed the sad fact that so many churches are not filling their Jerusalem with anything. So many churches not only have not turned the world upside down, they are not even able to stay alive themselves. Any church that is not winning people to Jesus Christ will die. It is inevitable. If a church cannot point to a single person it has won to Christ out of that "pagan pool" we call the world about us, that church is dying.

The preceding chapters have dealt at length with forming an organization which will help any church win people to the Lord. Theoretically, any person ought to be able to go out and win a few people to Jesus on his own in a year's time. But, if churches hope to grow, they will have to win more than one or two a year, for usually they will lose that many by death or by people moving away. It should be remembered that the simple formula for growth is to win more than are lost each year. The rate of growth will be determined by how many more are won.

The organization must be properly used if it is going to effectively contribute to the goal of winning the lost. This means planning everything with this in mind. Take revivals, for example. The average small church fails to have a real revival because they have no attendance during the week-night services of that revival. I have preached hundreds of times in services in small churches to a bunch of empty pews. It doesn't matter what is preached or who the preacher is if there is no one there to hear him. The revival ends. The pastor and congregation are disappointed. The evangelist is frustrated. Then people begin to say, "The day of revivals is over." I only wish the days of that kind of revival were over. But we go on trying to get empty pews converted and blaming one another because things are not like they used to be.

The organization of the church should be so put together that it all works for the common goal of adding to the Body of Christ. This means that everything done will have to be pulling in the same direction. The following are some suggestions when revival times come to help put the organization to the harness to pull for revival: Get all of these small groups praying for revival. Have each night allotted to some group. Have a night when the Caravan or Scouts are honored. Have them wear their uniforms; give some special recognition to them; get their parents there to see it happen. Have a night for the junior choir. Build it up with the younger set; their aunts, uncles, and grandparents will want to hear the children sing. All of these things bring people to revivals. The potential in this area is endless. But you have to plan for the organization to help have revival.

Only eternity will reveal how many people have been saved because they came to church for some special event with other members of the family. Or, perhaps it was a vacation Bible school closing program that brought someone in. One secret of getting people to respond to our invitation is this: We have to be specific. If we just invite people to church, they will reply most of the time, "Oh, sure, I will come some Sunday." But some Sunday just never arrives. But if you explain, "Our church is in a revival. Tomorrow night we will have our primary choir singing. Your granddaughter is in that group. Wouldn't you like to come hear her sing?" What will likely happen? They may still not come, but you certainly have a lot more clout when you have something special to which to invite them.

You can make the obvious application to every other organization in the whole structure of your church. But the point is, the organization of a "properly put together church" will help if it is harnessed up in the right way.

11
Organize for Outreach and Evangelism

A small group of men and women who are in training for presenting the gospel on a one-to-one basis meet on a regular basis. I invited a lady whom I won to the Lord about six months ago to speak to the group. She was very timid and retiring. But we were moved to tears as we sat around in a circle and heard her tell how happy she was to find something she had been seeking for 16 years. The joy that she and her husband found as they prayed while kneeling near the coffee table in their living room spilled over into the lives of everyone in the group. How can anyone criticize something that is bringing people to such a marvelous experience of saving grace? Others in that group reported winning a total of four people to Christ the night before. It was a precious time of sharing in the victories won for the week.

It is well known that people converted to Christ will not all automatically come to the church that was the instrument of their salvation. A good follow-up program will help bring them into the church. This means that the church will have to develop trained workers who go back with a Bible study program and some Christian nurturing. The new converts will have to be encouraged to come to church and get involved in some of the small-group activities. They will have to be brought into the public worship service and made to feel comfortable and at home. Then and only then will the church show evidence of growth.

BROADENING THE SPHERE OF INFLUENCE

Some churches stay small because they have influence with such a small number of people. Naturally, we want and try to get everyone to come to church on a regular basis. But every church needs a wide border of people who are friends of the church. We sometimes call them fringe people. But regardless of what they are called, every church needs all the friends it can get.

This sphere of influence is a two-way street. The church can help them, and they can help the church. Each church can help their people in some obvious ways. They are a very important part of the "fields [that] are white already to harvest" that Jesus spoke of in John 4:35. But there are many ways they can help the church. One way is that they become part of the mailing list. Every businessman who uses direct mailing knows how important that list is. And some of the radio and TV preachers have huge mailing lists. Financial appeals are made in this way. Support for all kinds of projects are made by this method. Churches in building programs find support in selling bonds here, or support for selling pews. What a long list could be made for reasons to build the fringe element of the church.

The problem is that most small churches have a very small fringe. Some have almost none. About the only influence some churches have is over the little handful who attend their services. The potential for growth in this type of church is very low.

How can we broaden the sphere of influence of the church? Well, we have to work at it. The old expression we used to use when I was a young Christian was "Get in, get out, or get run over." That sounds fine. The only trouble was that more got out than got in, and now we are not running over anybody. We should make every effort to get men saved. I am not advocating a soft pedal here. But we should not go at it in such a way that we wind up running more people away than we reach. If we cannot get them saved today, let us not close the door for tomorrow. Let us at least keep them friendly to our church.

A great source of potential for any church is the relatives and friends of new converts. When a person is first saved, most of his friends will be outside the church. But we had better reach them the first year after their conversion. The longer people are in the church, the fewer friends they have in the world, and the more they have in the church. This principle is also true of the relatives of the newly saved. They will usually have no fewer relatives two years after conversion, but the relationships may not be as close. In other words, things will polarize between them and their relatives.

Some will be impressed by a relative's newfound faith. That is the time to reach those relatives. But a year or so later it will be much harder to bring these same relatives under the influence of the church. This is not always true, but it works that way more than half the time. However, any show of interest should be followed up. The church should keep them on the mailing list and the visitation list. Who knows? We saw a man converted in a recent revival who had been around our church for over 30 years. His sister is a faithful member of our church. But this is an exception and not the rule.

One's own congregation is the greatest source of potential growth if their friends are seen as the harvest field. The people they work with, the people they attend school with, their next-door neighbors, their acquaintances; all of these are avenues to the hearts of people. But it is necessary for the laypeople to be trained to recognize these grand opportunities and take advantage of them while they are available.

I read in someone's newsletter this story. A church member came out one Sunday morning on his way to church just as his neighbor came out with golf clubs on his way for the Sunday game.

The golfer said to the Christian neighbor, "Come go with me for a game of golf." The Christian replied in a rather insulted manner that he did not play golf on Sunday and gave some other remarks about people who desecrated the Lord's day in such a fashion.

Then the golfer said, "You know, Henry, this is the seventh time I have invited you to go play golf with me. You have never one time invited me to go to church with you."

There it is. That is just about the way so many church members are reacting to the unsaved today. We condemn their wrong but make little or no effort to show them the right. And then we sit around and spend time and money studying why churches do not grow. How much better it would be if we taught our people how to win the lost rather than condemn them.

Everyone in your church has a few friends and relatives that are unsaved. Make a list of these with their help. Get them to pray for those on the list. Make them aware of their responsibility for those they know are unsaved. Help them to see that if they do not assume responsibility for reaching their own friends and relatives, no one else will. This concept must not only be preached and taught, but it must be emphasized continually. People are so quick to forget what is not mentioned frequently from the pulpit.

A REDUNDANCY SYSTEM

The people who put the man on the moon came up with something every church also needs. When I was visiting the Space Center in Houston, the man who was showing us around said that the whole complex system was almost foolproof. The reason was this. If one system failed, there was another backup system that did the same job. If this system also failed, there was a third that took over the same operation. So one system after another was available as a substitute in the event of failure. There were sometimes as many as seven backup systems. The chance of that many failures was very remote.

Now visitation is a drag in just about every church I have seen. Even most pastors, if they would admit it, are too slow here. Occasionally there will be some happy extrovert who thoroughly enjoys going from house to house day after day. But most people, pastors included, find it difficult. Most visitation programs are a farce. Very few church members ever do much visiting in behalf of the church.

Organization can help churches overcome this problem in a very simple and practical way. Sunday School teachers should visit and stay in contact with their class members. Many don't. But here is where the backup system begins to work. The Circle of Concern leaders are also doing the same thing. The Caravan leaders are also working with and visiting their people. Every group is busy with its own responsibility. When one person fails, another is there doing essentially the same thing. The feedback to the pastor from all of this is terrific. The people actually are taking care of one another. When the whole system is functioning as it should, the necessity of a lot of visitation is greatly reduced. This allows the pastor to concentrate on the cases that really need a pastor's care. He is not tied down visiting chronic absentees and a lot of people who probably will not be very responsive anyway.

Another element that comes out of this approach is this. Most of the people are so excited and involved that church attendance remains remarkably consistent. Naturally, there will be some attrition. These the pastor will have time to visit and work with. But this problem is greatly reduced.

With even limited efficiency on the part of leaders of each small group, the sheer number of people working with the same individuals insures some expression of concern from their church on a continuing basis. If the junior choir director fails to tell the pastor that Mary is sick, then the children's church director will be in touch with the family anyway. The Sunday School teacher may fail to contact Johnny who was sick last week, but the Caravan director didn't. Does this describe how well this can be made to work? Then if the pastor is on his toes, something good will just have to happen in that church.

12

Why Should Anyone Attend Your Church?

Several years ago (1957) Wesley Shrader wrote an article for *Life* magazine entitled "Our Troubled Sunday Schools." It became better known as, "The Most Wasted Hour of the Week." It stirred the expected response in sermons, articles, and books in defense of the Sunday School that had been so attacked. But in a short time it was all forgotten. Most of us went right on having about the same kind of Sunday Schools that we had before. But, for some at least, there was the haunting thought that the author of that article stirred such a defensive response because he came too close for comfort. While I would never call an hour spent studying the Bible, however poorly it is done, the most wasted hour, I certainly think we could improve on what a lot of Sunday Schools are doing. If we are really honest, I believe most Christians will have to admit that Sunday School is not always the high point of our week. It can be, and it should be; but judging by the number of "nodders" I have seen in some classes, we have quite a way to go to achieve this goal.

Why should anyone come to your church or Sunday School? Yours is probably not the only one in town. Denominational loyalty no longer seems to be sufficient. Convenience of location is no longer a prime factor. Most people have automobiles. When the list is complete, we still have a question that is painful. It is really hard to find many good reasons other than the one basic response: "People go to the church they do because they find there something that meets a basic need in their lives."

Sometimes family ties bring people to church. But then they move away from the old hometown, and there goes another reason. In the new city where they move, they look for a church to attend. They will probably go first to the denomination they used to attend. This is not always true, but it is frequently the case. When they arrive, the old friends are not there to greet them. Mom and Dad are not sitting up front on the left. The pastor is a stranger. That church had better have something to offer that family, or they may well start looking around for a church that does. That church had better make these new people feel welcome, needed, and at home if they hope to keep them coming. It could be presumptuous to assume that anyone should *automatically* come to that church.

How then can we create a situation that will keep people coming? All that has been stated so far is, in part, an answer to this question. But there is more.

First, we must get out of the rut and stay out. Getting out is hard enough, but staying out of a rut is even harder. The problem with this matter of the rut is that we don't know when we are in one. It is very hard to see ourselves as others see us. We think things are going along fine. We are comfortable and happy, the church is running smoothly, and everybody seems very pleased. If this sounds like your church, believe me, you are in a rut.

Making changes are painful and will be resisted. Well-meaning people will see any change as a threat to their security. Since the results of a major change are not wholly predictable, some will fear the consequences. Every church will have a few people who are asleep, and they will resist anyone disturbing their slumber.

But if we think getting out of a rut is hard, it is even more difficult to try to keep out of that rut. Most people drive their automobiles on nice paved roads with smooth surfaces. But a few who read these lines will remember driving on old dirt roads. These roads would develop ruts after there was some traffic. Some will also remember how the automobile would just naturally head for that rut. Keeping the front wheels out of the rut required some driving skill unknown to the average driver today.

There are still some cotton fields down south. We have some cotton produced very near our church here in Valdosta, Ga. There is a story that is told about old John who was a cotton farmer, as was his father and grandfather before him. One day when John went to the bank to borrow the money with which to do his planting, he was told by the banker something like this:

"John, the bank can't let you have any more money. You have lost money every year. The mortgage now is more than the farm is worth."

John asked, "What am I going to do? I can't plant without that loan."

"Well, I am sorry," the banker told him. "But the board met and said you would just have to get your money from some other source. Go see what you can do and stop back by late this afternoon," he concluded.

Well, old John went all over the little town with no success. So late in the afternoon just before closing time he went back to the bank and told his sad story.

"John, I'll tell you what we are going to do. The bank board said that if you will do exactly what we say for the next few years, we will finance you," declared the banker.

Not having much choice, old John agreed. He was told that he would have to plant peanuts and soya beans instead of cotton. The first year was a good year. The second was even better. In about four years John went back to the bank to see how things were coming.

"John, I have some good news for you," the banker exclaimed. "You are out of debt and on your own."

John stood there hardly able to believe what he was hearing. "You mean I am free of debt and on my own?" he queried. "Thank the Lord, now I can go back to planting cotton."

Keeping the church out of the rut and doing the things that work will not be as easy as one might think. There will always be some that pine for the good old days, even when those good old days produced nothing.

The *second* thing that a church will have to do is to generate some enthusiasm. Maybe people ought not to require it to keep them going, but the fact is that they do. Exciting services that are a celebration of the goodness of God will attract people. The public services must have the "upbeat" rather than a pessimistic "downbeat." People are put down and pushed aside all week. On Sunday they are looking for something that will lift them. Yes, I know we have to preach on sin and the evils of our day. We have to preach on the negatives and all of that. But if that is all we preach on, we will find ourselves preaching it to the walls.

We have all heard the story about the church on fire drawing a crowd. My story is real. Several years ago on a cold February morning at 4:00 A.M., the parsonage phone rang. The voice on the other end of the line informed me that my church was on fire. In fact, the lady said she could see the flames coming through the roof at that time. Needless to say, the next few minutes were busy minutes for us. When I arrived, two big fire engines had the street blocked, so I had to run up the hill on foot. When I arrived and told the firemen I was the pastor, they let me approach the building. Although it was a very cold morning and still not 5:00 A.M., quite a crowd of neighbors had gathered around.

In the few moments that I stood there before I was

permitted to enter the rear of the church building, a ridiculously funny thought passed briefly through my mind. Yes, just like the story went—when the church is on fire, it always draws a crowd. It wasn't very funny when we saw the damage, nor do we advocate such methods for crowd getting; but it did work.

Excitement is attractive. If church members are excited about their church, others will come to see why. If the pastor is not excited and the members seem bored or indifferent, there is little incentive for visitors to return. There are too many other churches around today that are excited about what they are doing. I would never remain as pastor of a church that did not excite me. It is not fair to the church or the pastor's ministry. This is one of the reasons I always insist on visiting a church and preaching for them before I accept a call as pastor. I don't go with the feeling that I am on trial, though I am; the converse is also true—they are too. If they don't excite me, then they don't need me as their pastor. It's a two-way street.

Now we are not talking about emotionalism or working up excitement just for excitement's sake. I have been in services where the pastor or evangelist was just trying to get the people excited. This can be done and is sometimes done just for a good show. This is not what is meant. But those who are genuinely excited about Jesus Christ and His saving grace have something to be enthusiastic about. If the gospel message is worth telling at all, it certainly is worthy of our most joyful expression of that message. If people can't get excited about the prospects of having eternal life, then I don't know what they would get excited about.

There is a *third* element that is equally important. We must be totally committed if we hope to even do anything worthwhile. Festus called the apostle Paul mad. The 120 disciples who came from the Upper Room on the Day of Pentecost were called drunk. Some of the names used to describe us in the early days of our own church were not very complimentary either. But they were doing something we are no longer doing today.

Being totally committed to the task is a critical point. Many get off to a good start, but few finish the race. Everyone knows that the first year the new pastor is at the church is called the "honeymoon." Everybody is behind him. He gets many invitations out to dinner. The members speak well of his sermons. The whole church is on its best behavior. But unfortunately it usually does not last. Soon the church will slump back into the old ruts it has been in for years. The old grievances will surface again. People cannot go on playing a role forever; eventually they become themselves again.

After the pastor has been at this church for a year or so, he begins to see the people as they really are. Then, and only then, can he help them be the kind of Christians they ought to be. It is at this point that the depth of commitment is really put to the test. It is then that the pastor will do his best work—after the honeymoon.

13
Finally, Brethren . . .

The complete verse found in 2 Thess. 3:1 reads, "Finally, brethren, pray for us, that the word of the Lord may have free course, and be glorified, even as it is with you." This last chapter on prayer is by no means an afterthought. It is placed last in the hope that its impression will linger as we go about building the Lord's Church.

The blunt words of Jesus as He came to the end of His earthly ministry must have continued ringing in the disciples' ears. He had told them, "Without me ye can do nothing" (John 15:5). Oh, it's not that we don't try. We are forever rushing out into our day without taking time to pray. We use the excuse that we didn't have time or there was an emergency. We had time to eat breakfast and do the other things we usually do every morning, but we let Satan trick us into thinking that we didn't have time to pray. The day ends in failure or frustration, and we wonder why. When will we ever learn that we can never do in the flesh the things that God said we could only do in the Spirit?

Our church had been going along smoothly for

some time. We had had some successes and some victories. But all of a sudden we bogged down. Finances got tight. Everything seemed too hard to get done. Critical attitudes began surfacing. Church growth was leveling off. Revivals were no longer productive. What was wrong? Well, we all did some soul searching. One day while I was praying in the study, the words "Without me ye can do nothing" came to me with a force that was more than audible. That was it! We had been working so hard. But the trouble was, we had been working all alone.

The resulting sermon I preached about the importance of prayer and the folly of laboring in the flesh exploded in the church like a bomb. We began a program of real prayer. The results were both instant and dramatic. Things began to happen all around us. As we prayed, we wondered: Why didn't we do this sooner? Why did we try everything else first?

It was not that our people had not been praying in the normal way that every Christian must pray. I am sure that most of them had some kind of private devotional life. I am sure that many of them had not abandoned the family altar. We still had Wednesday night prayer meeting. We even had prayer groups that met in the homes. We had about everything that most Christian congregations have. But we did not have the burden of prayer that is necessary to pray things to pass. Nor had we been conscious of the things that God wanted to do for us. He was only waiting on us to ask Him.

We started with the church directory. On Wednesday night we started praying for everyone by name who was listed in the directory. One by one we called their names at the throne of grace. Those who were the focal point of the prayers of the church were prayed for daily until the next Wednesday night prayer service. We usually took about 10 families at a time as the subject of our prayers. People knew that on a given week the whole church would be praying for them. And things began to happen to some of these families. Some who were unsaved were converted. God began to work among these families in a way that would have never been possible otherwise.

We took the Sunday School rolls down and read the names of every individual one at a time. We prayed for them individually. We prayed for the Circles of Concern. We prayed for the Sunday School teachers, the board members; we prayed for everyone who had any connection with our church. And as we prayed, there came into our church a sweet spirit of love and cooperation. Everyone sensed that we had found a forgotten source of power and blessing.

In the final analysis it will not matter how much organization we have. It will not matter how hard we work or how many hours we put in on the job. It will not matter how much money we raise or how many buildings we build. Statistics and graphs and charts will not be very important in the end if that is all we have to show for our efforts. The success of any church can never really be measured by the standards of men. These are about the only things we talk about when we get together and talk shop. If we don't know how to lay our burdens at the feet of Jesus, we are not going to do much that will be lasting in this world. If we pastors cannot or will not teach our people to pray as Jesus taught His disciples to pray, we will have continual experiences like the one recorded in Luke 9:37-42 and Matt. 17:14-21. And we will doubtless continue asking the same question they asked, "Why could not we cast him out?"

Some years ago I was conducting a revival in a major Southern city. The church placed me in a motel and made arrangements for me to eat in the restaurant connected with the motel. Since I did not have my automobile but was traveling by plane, that seemed an excellent arrangement. Things went fine for a few days. Then one day at noon I walked up to the door of the restaurant but found it locked. I saw people moving around inside and thought the door had been locked by accident. So I knocked as loudly as you can knock on a big glass door. No one paid much attention. But I kept it up. Finally someone came to the door and told me they were closed.

"What do you mean, closed?" I asked with a genuine feeling of shock. "It's lunchtime."

They were not very much interested in talking to me. I could see that something was wrong on the inside. Finally, they reluctantly told me that the cook had quit.

"But what am I going to do?" I queried. "I have no car to go some other place. It is too far to walk. Can't you fix me something? Do you have any leftovers?"

In pity, I suppose, they finally opened the door and

let me in. I ate what was surely leftovers. In fact, it had been left over for some time. But as I sat there eating what I could get, I looked out the window at the big sign that gave the name of the restaurant. And right there on the sign were the words "Fine Home Cooked Food."

On my way back to my room I had this lingering thought: DON'T ADVERTISE WHAT YOU CAN'T PROVIDE!